Make A List

WORDS AND IDEAS TO SUPPORT WRITING

By Nancy Hanssen and Kim Scattareggia
Grades K-1

Published by
Teaching Resource Center
14525 SW Millikan, #11910 Beaverton, OR 97005-2343
www.trcabc.com

Acknowledgments

We would like to acknowledge the many children with whom we have had the pleasure to work, and who helped us gain insight into the minds and hearts of young writers.

Published by
Teaching Resource Center
P.O. Box 82777, San Diego, CA 92138
www.trcabc.com

Edited by: Laura Woodard
Illustrations and design by: Linda Starr and Sharrie Bettencourt

©2005 Teaching Resource Center
All Rights Reserved.
Permission is granted to individual classroom teachers to reproduce portions of this book for classroom use only.

PRINTED IN THE UNITED STATES OF AMERICA

Table of Contents

Introduction 3
Sample Lessons 9

September 11
  September Words 11
  School Words 12
  Classroom Words 13
  Family Words 14
  Gingerbread Man Words . . . 15
  Classmates' Names 16
  Color Words 17
  Shape Words 18

October 19
  October Words 19
  Fall Words 20
  Apple Words 21
  Halloween Words 22
  Spider Words 23
  Pumpkin Words 24

November 25
  November Words 25
  Community Words 26
  Thanksgiving Words 27
  Mayflower Words 28
  Turkey Words 29
  Food Words 30
  Number Words 31

December 32
  December Words 32
  Winter Words 33
  Christmas Words 34
  Santa Words 35
  Toy Words 36
  Hanukkah Words 37
  Home Words 38

January 39
  January Words 39
  Snow Words 40
  Arctic Words 41
  Whale Words 42
  Martin Luther King Words . . 43
  Transportation Words 44
  Size Words 45

February 46
  February Words 46
  Valentine's Day Words 47
  Friend Words 48
  Feelings Words 49
  Post Office Words 50
  Abraham Lincoln Words . . . 51
  George Washington Words . 52

continued to next page

Table of Contents

March.................53
   March Words............53
   Spring Words...........54
   Weather Words.........55
   Kite Words.............56
   St. Patrick's Day Words.....57
   Green Words...........58
   Rainbow Words..........59

April...................60
   April Words.............60
   Easter Words...........61
   Egg Words.............62
   Bunny Words...........63
   Farm Words............64
   Farm Animal Words......65
   Pet Words.............66

May....................67
   May Words.............67
   Mother's Day Words......68
   Job Words.............69
   Plant Words............70
   Vegetable Words........71
   Zoo Words.............72
   Zoo Animal Words.......73

June...................74
   June Words............74
   Summer Words.........75
   Beach Words...........76
   Sea Life Words..........77
   Insect Words...........78
   Father's Day Words......79

July....................80
   July Words.............80
   Fourth of July Words......81
   Fruit Words............82
   Bear Words............83
   Camping Words.........84

August.................85
   August Words..........85
   Vacation Words.........86
   Dinosaur Words........87
   Five Senses Words.......88
   My Body Words.........89

Why Writer's Workshop in Kindergarten?

Before we implemented Writer's Workshop, our students didn't begin writing until several months into the school year. By then, we believed the children were ready to write. Our writing curriculum consisted of teacher-modeled lessons, language experience stories, and learning the names and sounds of the alphabet. By reading aloud on a regular basis we provided the children with background knowledge for eventual writing. We often felt we had to provide story starters in order to guide the children to a focused writing topic. We found ourselves asking our students the dreaded question, "What would you like to write about today?" We knew that we would often be faced with the inevitable answer, "I don't know." Our writing lessons seemed disconnected and contrived.

We were frustrated. We knew that we weren't getting the quality of writing we had hoped for even though our efforts were well intended. Observing Writer's Workshop in other grades and reading about the writing process, we asked ourselves a fundamental question: What does it mean to be "ready to write"?

The young children who enter our kindergarten classrooms have already had many experiences with print. Most parents read bedtime stories to their children and encourage them to interact with books. Young children see their parents reading the newspaper, writing notes or composing email messages. These children have noticed print in the environment and have made a connection between the written word and its meaning. The word *stop* on a street sign indicates an action. The name of a restaurant is identified with a place to enjoy a favorite meal. A child draws a picture and tells a story about it. These experiences are connections between oral language, the printed word and interactions with the world around them. Already the seeds for writing have been sown.

Writing doesn't wait until a child can hold a pencil or identify the letters of the alphabet. A picture or a scribble holds meaning for that child just as it does for the child who can write a few letters and words. Children are 'ready to write' the minute they walk through our classroom door.

We realized that we had to overcome the boundaries our own notions about writing readiness had created. Our task was to create an environment that encouraged and supported the link between oral language and the writing process. We embraced the understanding that the writing process includes both modeled writing and student engagement. We knew that we needed a simple, manageable routine. We also knew that we needed to commit a block of time in order to make sure all children were able to proceed through all of the stages of writing. We also wanted to organize and integrate our mini-lessons with other content areas. Once we freed ourselves, we were able to do the same with our students.

Now we begin writing the first week of school. We call our students writers. We encourage thoughts and ideas. We engage students in conversations that revolve around their experiences. We support all attempts at writing. We celebrate the writing process and devote as much time to writing as we do to reading and math.

What Is Writer's Workshop?

- Writer's Workshop is a philosophy that oral language development and print are strongly connected. It supports this connection by providing children with many opportunities to engage in conversations about their ideas for writing.

- Writer's Workshop builds upon the child's thoughts, ideas, and interests relative to their own life experiences.

- Writer's Workshop provides children with a daily block of time devoted to the writing process.

- Writer's Workshop is a process within an environment that supports, encourages and celebrates writing at all stages of development.

Getting Started

The first step is to take a deep breath. Then, prepare the classroom with the necessary tools for Writer's Workshop and set up a routine. The biggest leap is to just begin. The environment might be hectic for the first four to six weeks. Don't give up, even on those challenging days. Once you begin to see children's ideas blossom into print and hear their excitement about writing, you and your students will feel empowered. Like anything, the routine will become automatic. It takes time and patience.

Allow for a forty-five minute time block for Writer's Workshop. If you schedule it before a snack, lunch or recess break, you can use the break to prepare the five pieces of writing to be published and illustrated the following day.

What Tools Do I Need?

To effectively model the writing process you must have a comfortable setup. Have a solid easel that can support a large tablet of chart paper. Make sure you have a comfortable chair that allows easy access to the chart and allows you to interact with the children. The use of chart paper is important so that you can keep a record of writing lessons. Use these saved writing lessons for rereading, reviewing previous teaching points or continuing with a story idea.

- Use colored markers to highlight teaching points and vocabulary, and to illustrate your writing.

- Make various pointers available as a fun way to direct children to print, to highlight teaching points and for rereading.

- For each modeled writing lesson, preplan what you will write about and where you want to take your students with this idea. The *Make A List* word lists will assist you with a sample piece of writing and accompanying words. The lists encourage ideas, concepts and vocabulary development. They also give the children support with spelling during the writing process. Make the list of words visible in the classroom, perhaps in a large pocket chart, and provide copies of the list for the students. Have the students store the lists in the tubs at their tables for further reference.

Using the Word Lists

The ability to create ideas is central to writing, and the development of vocabulary is a necessary component. The beginning writer needs support to generate ideas and build background knowledge and vocabulary prior to writing. Like word walls and personal dictionaries, *Make A List* word lists give beginning writers a tool that will help them effectively and independently engage in the writing process. The word lists also provide the beginning writer with a semantic organizer to assist in the development of concepts and comprehension. As an added benefit they help free you to work with small groups or individual students during the writing process.

We built the word lists around our monthly units of study to integrate with social studies, math and science. By connecting the curriculum to Writer's Workshop, our teaching is more effective, the curriculum is extended and children have a context for writing.

The words are arranged in random order but those that begin with the same letter/sound or that are visually similar are not placed together. In this way, children can begin to use their knowledge of letters and sounds to differentiate between words. Using the word lists on a daily basis builds the familiarity of the vocabulary for children.

- Use multiple copies of the word lists with the whole class, small groups or individual students.

- Place the lists in tubs for small groups of students or at the writing center.

- Send home copies of the lists and encourage parent support in the writing process.

What Tools Do Students Need?

- Set up your classroom with tables to accommodate four groups of five children. At each of the tables, have tubs for pencils, erasers, word lists, ABC cards and sentence frames.

- Make copies of sentence frames available in each tub. Sentence frames often help students get a jump-start with their writing and free you to help students during their writing time. Beginning writers often use "I love…", "I like to…", "I have…", and "I am going to…"

- Each child needs his or her own journal. Journals can be composition books, spiral notebooks or paper stapled together. Depending on the needs of the student, some may begin with lined paper, while others who are developing fine motor control may require blank paper. Keep the journals in two different tubs: the "Finished" tub and the "TBC" (To Be Continued) tub. After each modeled writing lesson, personally distribute the journals and have a quick conversation with the child about what he or she is going to write that day. If a child can't give you a writing topic, it usually means that he or she may need inspiration from peers to help with the decision. Wait and ask again after distributing a few more journals and hearing more ideas. This conversation is valuable as it helps students focus and gives them a running start on their writing for the day. It builds the pathway between oral and written communication.

Publishing Student Writing

Publishing can go very quickly with young children. Each day pre-select five children who will have their work edited, copied and published. Edit the children's writing and re-write it on large white sheets of 12" by 18" construction paper. Begin with a layout that resembles text in books: writing on the bottom of the page and illustrations on the top. Later on in the year, vary the layout on the pages, use smaller paper and consider using a printer or word processor.

To keep motivated children need to see a book of their published work within a reasonable time so they can experience writing for an audience. Have a list of your students and daily keep track of whose work has been published. We like to have each student make a book after his or her writing has been published four times, or about once a month. We have a clothesline around the room with designated spaces for each child's published work. The displayed work gives students a sense of pride and serves as reading material for children in "read around the room" activities.

Use the published work as the pages of the book. Again, keep it simple. For the front and back cover of the book children select from an assortment of colored 12" by 18" construction paper. Staple the pages together, fold and staple over them a colored piece of drawing paper and cut a binding using various shaped scissors. Later on in the year you can introduce smaller paper and even bind books with a bookbinding machine.

Title the book, add the name of the student writer and have him or her illustrate it. Place the finished book in your classroom library. After a few weeks, transfer the book into the child's personal reading box and later send it home. Parents treasure these books.

What Publishing Tools Do Students Need?

- Set up a table for publishing with a variety of materials available for children who are illustrating their piece of writing.

- During the first two months of publishing the written work, keep the art materials fairly consistent. Include crayons, colored pencils and colored markers.

- Motivate your students by adding new materials throughout the year, such as different-sized paper, glitter pens, watercolors, stickers, tempera paint and sponge painting.

Modeled Writing Lesson

Because children enter school with thoughts, ideas and experiences related to their family, home and neighborhood, the *Make a List* word lists for the beginning of the school year build on these experiences. They aim to broaden a young child's experiences and expand his or her ideas for writing.

Select Literature or Personal Connection

Select a title that highlights a theme or idea for writing. Or, choose a theme to discuss that relates to a shared item, a personal event or a classroom experience.

Lead a Conversation

- Read a story and then discuss an aspect of the book you wish to highlight. Use it as a springboard for writing. Model the thinking process for children. A possible starter might be "This story reminds me of…"

- While discussing the story or theme, ask questions and pose thoughts that lead students to your predetermined idea for writing for that day. This process helps children talk about their own related experiences. When it comes time to write, begin with the question "What am I going to write about today?" Then follow up with "I have an idea…"

You will begin to hear children use this same language as they converse about their own writing. Students prompt and support each other by saying, "What are you going to write about today?" or "I have an idea for you." These conversations begin to build a community of writers.

Model Writing in the Class Journal

Before you begin the modeled writing process, introduce the word list. Read through the list and then say, "Do we see some words that we know? I think I will begin my writing using this word from the list." Choose a word that will generate the most ideas and provide teaching points. Together, compose a piece of writing using words from the list.

Model Teaching Points

Model the teaching points during the modeled writing lesson and reinforce them afterwards. Try to stick to one or two teaching points. These teaching points should be targeted towards the needs and strengths of your students based on your informal assessments, observations and anecdotal notes. Read and reread the piece of writing with your students.

Prepare to Write

Students sit knee-to-knee with a partner and talk about their writing idea for the day. This is when you hear children ask other children what they will write about and the responses, such as "I am going to write about my mom." This two- to three-minute conversation is valuable as it gives each child the opportunity to listen to others' ideas and in turn process, expand and refine his or her own. Don't skip this step.

Acknowledge Today's Published Writers

The five students who were selected to have their writing published share their writing. Edit and copy each piece of writing for its young author on 12" by 18" construction paper. Acknowledge the children's work with applause, a cheer and/or a drum-roll and send them off to the publishing table to illustrate their work.

Distribute Student Journals and Word Lists

As you hand out the journals, have each student quickly tell you his or her writing topic for the day. Allowing children to listen to each other as they tell you what they are going to write for the day also helps them with ideas for writing. This is also the time to distribute *Make A List* word lists.

Begin Student Writing Time

- Students return to the tables and begin to write in their journals. One group of students works independently at the publishing center.

- Facilitate the writing process by helping students or working with small groups.

- Students use the word lists, ABC charts, word walls and dictionaries to support independent writing.

Close

- Provide the students with a one-minute warning signal to give them time to complete their writing for the day.

- After an additional signal, have students put away their writing and publishing tools.

- If a student has not completed a piece of writing, he or she writes "TBC" (To Be Continued) at the top to indicate they need to return to that piece of writing the following day. A *Make A List* word list can be used to mark their place in their writing journal. The child then places his or her journal in the "TBC" tub. The students who have completed their written pieces place their journals in the "Finished" tub.

- Gather the students on the carpet.

- Select five journals from the "Finished" tub from which to have the day's writing published. Selecting these at the close of Writer's Workshop creates motivation and excitement, and makes it easier to keep track of which students still need to be published. Meet with the students selected when the others have been dismissed. Edit their writing and copy it onto the 12" by 18" construction paper for illustrating. You're ready for the next day.

Sample Lessons

The first half of each lesson provides the theme, book selection, modeled writing ideas and teaching points.

DAY 1

Theme: October
Literature Connection: *Owl at Home* by Arnold Lobel
Conversation: "Owl really likes the moon in the story. Have you noticed the moon this month? October is known for its big moon. Let's write about October. As we look at our October Word List, let's see if there are words we might need for writing today." (Everyone participates by showing thumbs up or down regarding each word choice.)
Modeled Writing: *In October the days get shorter and the weather gets chilly. The moon is big in the night sky. All month long I wait for the last day of October because it is Halloween!*
Teaching Points: "I hear the /m/ sound in the word moon. Who would like to come up and highlight the letter that makes that sound? As we reread today's entry, tell me the October list words we used that I can underline."

The second half of each lesson remains consistent after instruction of the daily teaching points.

Prepare to Write: "This list helped us write today's journal entry. Let's read the list words. Now it's time to think about what you would like to write about today. Would you like to write about today's topic or another subject, or would you like to continue with your TBC (To Be Continued) piece of writing? Share with a partner your idea for writing today."
Acknowledge Today's Published Writers: "Let's clap for today's published writers! I'll help them read their stories aloud and you think about how they might illustrate them." (The students, usually 4-5 each day, are dismissed to Publishing Table.)
Distribute Journals: "What are you planning to write about today?" (Distribute quickly, with plenty of supportive comments!)
Student Writing Time: (This is where we do mini-conferencing with our writers. We interact briefly offering suggestions, compliments and encouragement where needed. Remind students to use the tools around them such as word lists, word walls, sentence frames, dictionaries, and displayed published work.)
Closing: "In one minute Writer's Workshop will be over. Time to finish your last word. If you are not finished, use a TBC to mark your spot. Reread today's entry."
Turn In Journals: "Please turn in your journal; put it in the *correct* tub. One is for *unfinished* TBC entries and the other is for *finished* work you would like to publish."

DAY 2

Theme: Fall
Literature Connection: *When Autumn Falls* by Kelly Nidey
Conversation: "There were lots of references to the season of fall in this book. Can everyone think of three? Show me three fingers when you can. Let's share some signs of fall. Our fall word list has many of those same words you used. As we read our fall word list, think about if it would be a good choice for our writing today."
Modeled Writing in Class Journal: *There are signs of fall everywhere. The leaves are changing from green to red, yellow and brown. The weather is cooler and it is windy. Squirrels are busy hiding nuts.*
Teaching Points: "We used three color words in our journal today. Who sees all three?" (Allow a little time until all hands

are up.) "Who can highlight one of the color words and read it for us?" "As we reread our story, touch your eyes when you read a sight word we are learning and I will underline it."

DAY 3

Theme: Halloween
Literature Connection: *Clifford and the Halloween Parade* by Norman Bridwell
Conversation: "Clifford was a great addition to the parade in the book. Would you like to have a Halloween parade too? Let's check our Halloween list to see if it has some words we heard in the story. Be thinking about which of these we might use in our writing today."
Modeled Writing: *Halloween is October 31st. We will have a Halloween parade at school. I will wear my spooky spider costume for the parade. Then I am going trick-or-treating with my family.*
Teaching Points: "We know the sound /s/ is made with the letter 's'. Touch your ear if you hear a second sound when I say /sp/." (Repeat sound until entire class can identify the /sp/ sound.) "Who can help us find a word in our story with that sound?" (Volunteers highlight spooky and spider.) "As we reread today, help me find some list words we used in this entry."

DAY 4

Theme: Spiders
Literature Connection:
Spiders by Gail Gibbons
Conversation: "I learned a lot of spider facts from this book. Show me with your fingers how many new things you learned about spiders." (Offer hints for increased participation.) "Our spider word list will help you remember some of those facts. It will give us vocabulary for writing about spiders today. As we read, give a thumbs-up if you remember what the word means."
Modeled Writing: *Spiders are arachnids. Spiders have eight legs. They spin silk with their spinnerets and make fascinating webs. The tarantula is the biggest spider in the world!*
Teaching Points: "Yesterday we learned the sound that 's' and 'p' make when we put them together to make the blend /sp/. Today's entry has more /sp/ words. Be a detective and count how many /sp/ words you see. Show me with your fingers." (Volunteers highlight spiders, spin, and spinnerets.) "As we read today's entry, show me eight fingers every time we've used a word from the spider word list and I'll circle it and give it legs."

DAY 5

Theme: Pumpkins
Literature Connection: *Pumpkin Pumpkin* by Jean Titherington
Share a pumpkin with the class and have them vote to decide which type of face to carve on the pumpkin.
Conversation: "Pumpkins ripen this time of year, just in time for Halloween. In what other ways do we use pumpkins? Let's read our pumpkin word list and decide which words to use to help us write about pumpkins."
Modeled Writing: *Pumpkins are perfect for picking when they are big and orange. I like pumpkin pie, but I like to carve my pumpkin into a jack-o-lantern best of all. I think mine will have a scary face this year!*
Teaching Points: "Let's make the sound that the letter 'p' makes. Try writing it with your finger on the carpet or on your neighbor's back. Be a 'p' police and count how many 'p' words we used in our story today." (Volunteers highlight 'p' words.) "As we reread, help me locate and underline the sight words in our story."

September Words

school
fall
leaves
football
Labor Day
month
friends
weather
colorful
cool

Literature Connection
School Days by B.G. Hennessy
This Is the Way We Go To School
    by Edith Baer
Will You Be My Friend? by Eric Carle

Modeled Writing (sample)
In *September* we say goodbye to summer and hello to *fall*. This *month* the *weather* will cool off and the *leaves* will begin to turn colors and *fall* from the trees. In *school* I will meet new *friends*, like you!

Teaching Points
• *-all* words (fall, ball)
• Locate beginning /s/ sound
• Capitalize month names
• Locate/review list words
• Springboards for Writing

Springboards for Writing
In September I like to…
In September the weather…
This month I will…
School is…

School Words

teacher
classroom
playground
office,
secretary
principal
nurse
library
librarian
custodian

Literature Connection
First Day Hooray by Nancy Poydar
Mouse's First Day of School
   by Lauren Thompson
School Bus by Donald Crews

Modeled Writing (sample)
On the tour of our *school* we will see new people and places. In the *office* we can say hello to the *secretary*, the nurse and the *principal*. All these people make our *school* a special place to be!

Teaching Points
- *-an* words (ran, man)
- Review /highlight sight words
- Highlight list words
- Compound words (classroom, playground)

Springboards for Writing
On the playground I like to...
My teacher is...
The school is...
The principal is...
Nurses are...

Classroom Words

- tools
- supplies
- pencil
- pen
- crayon
- paint
- marker
- paper
- journal
- scissors
- backpack
- snack
- book
- computer

Literature Connection
First Day Jitters by Julie Dannenberg
Miss Bindergarten Gets Ready for Kindergarten by Joseph Slate
The Night Before Kindergarten by Natasha Wing
My First Day of School by Patrick K. Hallinan
Countdown to Kindergarten by Alison McGhee
Look Out Kindergarten, Here I Come by Nancy Carlson

Modeled Writing (sample)
We have many tools in our *classroom*. We use *crayons*, *markers* and *paper* for drawing. We write in our *journals*.

Teaching Points
• Beginning sounds of word list words
• Plurals (pen/pens)
• Review/highlight sight words

Springboards for Writing
I love to draw with…
In my backback I have…
I use scissors…

Family Words

- mom
- dad
- parents
- sister
- brother
- baby
- aunt
- uncle
- cousin
- grandma
- grandpa
- grandparents
- pet

Literature Connection
The Relatives Came
   by Cynthia Rylant
Just Me and My Little Brother
   by Mercer Mayer
Piggybook by Anthony Browne
Just Like My Dad by Tricia Gardella
William's Doll by Charlotte Zolotow
Song and Dance Man
   by Karen Ackerman
Julius the Baby of the World
   by Kevin Henkes
Mama, Do You Love Me?
   by Barbara M. Joosse

Modeled Writing (sample)
This weekend my relatives came for a visit. I saw my *aunt*, my *uncle* and my two *cousins*. We spent the day talking, laughing and sharing old *family* stories. It was wonderful to see my *family* again.

Teaching Points
- *-ing* ending usage
- Homonyms: to, two, too
- Review/highlight sight words

Springboards for Writing
My family likes to…
One time my (brother/sister)…
My mom makes the best…
My dad is good at…
I went with my family…

Gingerbread Man Words

- man
- boy
- woman
- oven
- cookies
- fox
- river
- swim
- farmer
- pig
- cat
- horse
- field

Literature Connection
The Gingerbread Boy by Paul Galdone
The Gingerbread Boy by Sue Kassirer
The Gingerbread Man
   by Eric A. Kimmel
The Gingerbread Man
   by Karen Schmidt

Modeled Writing (sample)
The *Gingerbread Boy* was so fast! He got away from everyone except the *fox*. I can see why the *fox* wanted to eat him. *Gingerbread cookies* are so yummy!

Teaching Points
- Short /o/ sound (got, fox)
- Highlight list vocabulary
- Review/highlight sight words
- Exclamation mark usage

Springboards for Writing
The Gingerbread Boy
Gingerbread cookies taste…
The fox was tricky because…
I like to run because…
One time I made cookies…

Classmates' Names

boys

girls

teacher

friends

class

_____

_____

_____

Literature Connection
Crysanthemum by Keven Henke
We Share Everything!
   by Robert N. Munsch
I Am Special by Kinberly Jordano
Look What I Can Do by Jose Aruego
We Can Share At School
   by Rozanne Lanczak Williams
Kindergarten Kids by Ellen Sensi

Modeled Writing (sample)
We have made many new *friends* in our *class*. There are almost as many *boys* as *girls*. Today *Alex, Nick, Zoe, Sarah* and *Taylor* are in the green row. They are great *friends*!

Teaching Points
- Name capitalization
- Comma usage
- Review/highlight sight words
- Highlight list words

Springboards for Writing
My teacher is…
I like to play with…
Reading is fun with…

Color Words

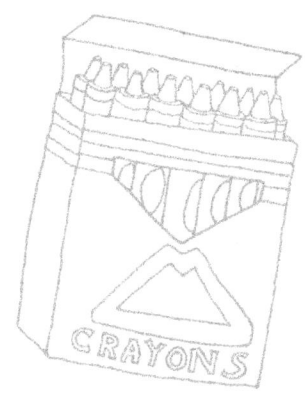

- red
- yellow
- blue
- green
- purple
- orange
- white
- black
- brown
- pink
- turquoise
- primary
- secondary

Literature Connection
Color Dance by Ann Jonas
Brown Bear, Brown Bear by Eric Carle
Mouse Paint by Ellen Stoll Walsh
Dogs Colorful Day by Emma Dodd
Is It Red? Is It Yellow? Is It Blue?
   by Tana Hoban

Modeled Writing (sample)
The three *primary colors* are *red*, *yellow* and *blue*. These can be mixed together to make other *colors*. *Yellow* and *blue* make *green*. *Red* and *blue* make *purple*. *Red* and *yellow* make *orange*. What is your favorite *color*?

Teaching Points
- *-ed* words (red, bed)
- Question marks
- Review/highlight sight words

Springboards for Writing
My favorite color is…
I love to paint…
I like to mix…
My crayon box has…

Shape Words

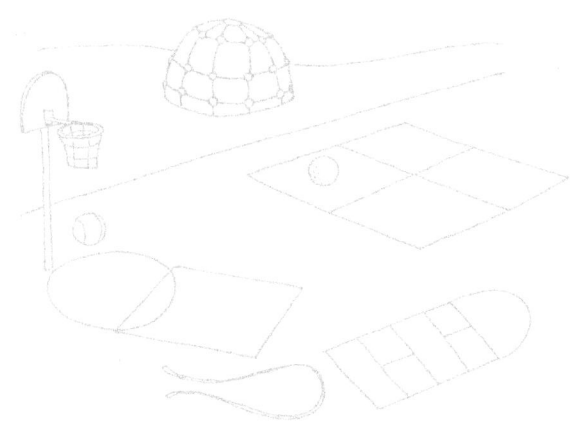

circle

round

square

rectangle

triangle

oval

diamond

cube

sphere

lines

curves

Literature Connection
Shapes, Shapes, Shapes
    by Tana Hoban
The Shape of Things
    by Dayle Ann Dodds
What Am I? Looking Through Shapes at Apples and Grapes
    by N.N. Charles

Modeled Writing (sample)
If you look around, you will see many different *shapes*. The sun is a large *round circle*. A book is a *square* or a *rectangle*. *Shapes* are all around us.

Teaching Points
- *-ape* words (shape, tape)
- *-ook* words (look, book)
- *-ound* (round, found)
- Review/highlight sight words

Springboards for Writing
A circle is...
There are squares...
I like to draw...
A diamond is like a...
The shape of...

October Words

fall
leaves
moon
orange
black
chilly
bats
month
Halloween
fun
scary
costume

Literature Connection
White Is the Moon by Valerie Greeley
Owl Moon by Jane Yolen
There's a Nightmare in My Closet
   by Mercer Mayer
Andrew's Amazing Monsters
   by Kathryn Hook Berlan

Modeled Writing (sample)
October is an exciting *month*. The days get shorter and the weather gets *chilly*. The *moon* is big in the night sky. All *month* long, I wait for the last day of *October* when *Halloween* comes!

Teaching Points
• Capitalize month names
• Initial sound /m/ and /h/
• Review/highlight sight words
• Highlight list words

Springboards for Writing
October will be…
The best thing about this month…
I like October because…
October is fun/scary because…

Fall Words

windy

harvest

chill

leaves

autumn

owl

squirrel

nuts

change

brown

red

yellow

moon

Literature Connection
Autumn Days by Ann Schweninger
Good Night Owl by Pat Hutchins
Nuts to You by Lois Ehlert
When Autumn Comes
   by Robert Maas
Sleepy Bear by Lydia Dobcovich

Modeled Writing (sample)
There are signs of *fall* everywhere. The leaves are *changing* from green to red, *yellow* and *brown*. The weather is cooler and it is *windy*. *Squirrels* are busy hiding *nuts* in the *fall*.

Teaching Points
- *-ing* endings
- *-all* words (fall, tall)
- Review/highlight sight words

Springboards for Writing
When the moon is full…
The trees look…
In fall the weather…
In fall I like to…

Apple Words

red
core
peel
seeds
stem
tree
yellow
green
fruit
sauce
pie
juice
bite

Literature Connection
Apple Pie Tree by Zoe Hall
My Apple Tree by Harriet Ziefert
The Seasons of Arnold's Apple Tree
　by Gail Gibbons
How Do Apples Grow?
　by Betsy Maistro
Johnny Appleseed by Steven Kellogg
Apples and Pumpkins
　by Anne Rockwell

Modeled Writing (sample)
Apples are one of my favorite *fruits*. I would like to pick one from the *tree* and take a big *bite*. I love to eat them in *apple pie* best of all!

Teaching Points
- Short /a/ sound
- Initial sounds /f/ and /b/
- Review/highlight sight words

Springboards for Writing
My favorite apple is…
Red apples taste…
Green apples taste…
My mom makes the best apple…

Halloween Words

- pumpkin
- jack-o-lantern
- costume
- ghost
- trick-or-treat
- carnival
- parade
- haunted house
- spider
- witch
- candy
- spooky

Literature Connection
Clifford and The Halloween Parade
   by Norman Bridwell
Space Case by Edward Marshall
Where the Wild Things Are
   by Maurice Sendak
Go Away Big Green Monster
   by Ed Emberley
Who Said Boo?
   by Nancy White Carlstrom

Modeled Writing (sample)
Halloween is October 31st. There is a *carnival* at school. The *haunted house* will be *spooky*. I will wear my *ghost costume* for the *Halloween parade*. I am going *trick-or-treating* with my family.

Teaching Points
- *-ick* words (trick, lick)
- *sp* blend (spooky, spider)
- *-ouse* words (house, mouse)
- Review/highlight sight words

Springboards for Writing
My Halloween costume…
Halloween is…
I will go trick-or-treating…
The school carnival…
Halloween is…

Spider Words

- arachnid
- web
- legs
- eight
- abdomen
- spinnerets
- silk
- egg sac
- fangs
- prey
- black widow
- tarantula

Literature Connection
The Very Busy Spider by Eric Carl
Spinning Spiders by Melvin Berger
Spiders by Gail Gibbons

Modeled Writing (sample)
Spiders are *arachnids*. *Spiders* have *eight legs*. They spin *silk* with their *spinnerets* and make beautiful *webs*. A *black widow* is a type of spider.

Teaching Points
- *sp* blend (spider, spinnerets)
- *-in* words (spin, tin)
- Review and highlight sight words

Springboards for Writing
Spiders are...
Spiders live...
Black widow spiders...
Once I saw a spider...
Tarantulas are so...

Pumpkin Words

- orange
- patch
- stem
- vine
- flower
- leaves
- seeds
- carve
- jack-o-lantern
- smooth
- round
- big
- small
- pie

Literature Connection
It's Pumpkin Time! by Zoe Hall
The Pumpkin Patch by Elizabeth King
Pumpkins by Mary Lyn Ray
Apples and Pumpkins
   by Anne Rockwell

Modeled Writing (sample)
Pumpkins are perfect for picking when they are *big* and *orange*. I like *pumpkin pie* but I like to *carve* my *pumpkin* into a *jack-o-lantern* best of all. I think mine will have a scary face this year!

Teaching Points
- Initial /p/ sound
- Color word review
- Review/highlight sight words
- Highlight list words

Springboards for Writing
Pumpkins make the best...
My jack-o-lantern will look...
My favorite pie is...
Pumpkin plants grow...

November Words

- fall
- leaves
- family
- visit
- cook
- Veterans' Day
- honor
- military
- Thanksgiving
- month
- feast
- turkey
- dinner

Literature Connection
Ox-Cart Man by Donald Hall
Popcorn Book by Tomie De Paola
Molly's Pilgrim by Barbara Cohen
What is Thanksgiving?
 by Harriet Ziefert
The Thanksgiving Story
 by Alice Dalgliesh

Modeled Writing (sample)
In *November*, we *honor* war *veterans* on *Veterans' Day*. We *visit* with *family*. We *cook* a big *turkey dinner* in celebration of *Thanksgiving Day*. We eat yummy pumpkin pie for dessert.

Teaching Points
- Capitalize month names
- Capitalize holiday names
- Review/highlight sight words
- Highlight list words

Springboards for Writing
In November, it is fun to…
We honor veterans because…
This month my family…

Community Words

- neighborhood
- homes
- fire station
- police station
- hospital
- post office
- library
- school
- park
- mall
- grocery store
- toy store
- pet store

Literature Connection
On My Street by Eve Merrian
On the Town: A Community Adventure by Judith Caseley
Richard Scarry's Busy Town by Richard Scarry
On Market Street by Arnold Lobel
City Mouse-Country Mouse and Two More Mouse Tales from Aesop by John Wallner
Mike Mulligan and His Steam Shovel by Virginia Lee Burton

Modeled Writing (sample)
There are many *homes* in our *neighborhood*. There is a *fire station* and a *library* too. Our *community* has a *park* where we can play. I like to go to the *toy store* at the *mall*.

Teaching Points
- *st* blend (store, station)
- *-oy* diphthong (toy, boy)
- *-all* words (mall, ball)
- Review/highlight sight words

Springboards for Writing
My neighborhood is…
Our family shops at…
I like to go to the…
We mail letters at the…
We visited the…

Thanksgiving Words

- family
- celebrate
- thankful
- feast
- dinner
- relatives
- turkey
- pumpkin pie
- tradition
- holiday
- Mayflower
- Pilgrims
- Indians

Literature Connection
Arthur's Thanksgiving by Marc Brown
Samuel Eaton's Day by Kate Waters
The Perfect Thanksgiving
   by Eileen Spinelli
Thanksgiving Is Here by Diane Goode
Today Is Thanksgiving!
   by P.K. Hallinan

Modeled Writing (sample)
Long ago the *Pilgrims* and *Indians* gave *thanks* for a bountiful harvest. Today *Thanksgiving* is celebrated with *family* and *friends*. We share a big *turkey dinner* with all the trimmings.

Teaching Points
- Capital letters of names/places (Pilgrims, Mayflower, Plymouth Rock)
- Clap multi-syllabic words (family, celebrate)
- Review/highlight sight words

Springboards for Writing
I am thankful for...
Thanksgiving is...
I love to eat...
My family...
For Thanksgiving...

Mayflower Words

- ship
- sails
- sailors
- Pilgrims
- England
- Atlantic Ocean
- land
- Plymouth Rock
- America
- Indians
- Squanto
- colony
- New England

Literature Connection
If You Sailed on the Mayflower by Ann McGovern
Sarah Morton's Day by Kate Waters
Eating the Plates: The Pilgrim Book of Food and Manners by Lucille Recht Penner
The Story of the First Thanksgiving by Elaine Raphael and Don Bolognese
Thanksgiving Day by Gail Gibbons

Modeled Writing (sample)
The *Mayflower* was the *ship* that brought the *Pilgrims* from *England* to *America*. They *sailed* across the *Atlantic Ocean* to reach the new *land*. The *Indians* lived there.

Teaching Points
- Capitalize names/places
- Clap multi-syllabic words
- Review/highlight sight words

Springboards for Writing
If I sailed on the Mayflower, I would…
Pilgrim life was hard, but…
Being a pilgrim would be…

Turkey Words

- birds
- gobble
- wattle
- wings
- feathers
- egg
- chick
- tom
- hen
- farm
- dinner
- drumstick
- delicious

Literature Connection
One Tough Turkey by Steven Kroll
A Turkey For Thanksgiving by Eve Bunting
Oh, What a Thanksgiving! by Steven Kroll
Sometimes It's Turkey, Sometimes It's Feathers by Lorna Balian
This Is the Turkey by Abby Levine
Don't Eat Too Much Turkey by Miriam Cohen

Modeled Writing (sample)
Turkeys are *funny birds*. They strut around showing their colorful *feathers*, saying *gobble gobble* to everyone! A *Turkey* hatches from an *egg* and grows up to be a *tom* or a *hen*.

Teaching Points
- *-en* words (hen, ten, men)
- Initial /t/ and /f/ sounds
- Review/highlight sight words
- Highlight list words

Springboards for Writing
Turkeys are…
We eat turkey for…
My mom makes turkey…

Food Words

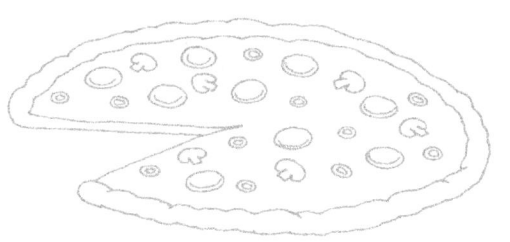

- pizza
- spaghetti
- vegetables
- fruit
- chicken
- fish
- hamburger
- sushi
- tortillas
- salad
- soup
- dessert

Literature Connection
Pete's a Pizza by William Steit
Wednesday is Spaghetti Day
  by Maryan Cocea-Leffler
The Story of Noodles
  by Ying Chang Compertine
Magda's Tortillas
  by Becky Chavarria-Chairez
Stone Soup by Ann McGovern
Gregory, the Terrible Eater
  by Mitchell Sharmat

Modeled Writing (sample)
My family eats different kinds of *food*. We like to make *pizza* together. On the weekend, we barbeque *hamburgers* and *chicken*. I make tasty *soup*, but my favorite *food* is *spaghetti*.

Teaching Points
- Compound words (hotdog, hamburger)
- Beginning sounds of words
- Review/highlight sight words

Springboards for Writing
My family loves to eat…
We love to cook…
My favorite food is…
My mom bakes…

Number Words

zero
one
two
three
four
five
six
seven
eight
nine
ten
fifty
hundred
million
infinity
count

Literature Connection
Six Crows by Leo Lionni
Over in the Meadow by Sharon O'Neil
Five Little Monkeys Jumping on the Bed by Eileen Christelow
Inch by Inch by Leo Lionni
1 Is One by Tasha Tudor
One Hundred Hungry Ants by Elinor Pinczes
Counting Crocodiles by Judy Sierra

Modeled Writing (sample)
In our classroom, I see *one* clock. I *count five* tables and *three* paint easels. There are *four* bookcases with *hundreds* of books. I see *zero* frowns and *twenty* beautiful smiles. *Counting* is fun!

Teaching Points
- *-ing* ending usage (count, counting)
- *cl* blend (clock, classroom)
- Review/highlight sight words
- Highlight word list

Springboards for Writing
My favorite number is...
My lucky number is...
I can count to...
Infinity means...

December Words

- winter
- snow
- decorate
- holiday
- Christmas
- Hanukkah
- family
- gifts
- guests
- toys
- month
- vacation

Literature Connection
Stories by Firelight by Shirley Hughes
Is That You, Winter?
   by Stephen Gammell
Lights of Winter: Winter Celebrations Around the World
   by Heather Conrad
The Tomten
   by Astrid Lindgren
Frozen Noses
   by Jan Carr

Modeled Writing (sample)
December is the busiest *month* of the year. My *family* spends time *shopping, decorating,* sending *cards,* and cooking. We enjoy preparing for our favorite *holiday* of the year.

Teaching Points
- Capitalize names/months
- *-ing* ending
- Review/highlight sight words
- Highlight list words

Springboards for Writing
This month my family…
In December we…
On our vacation we will…
If it snows I will…

Winter Words

- snow
- white
- snowflakes
- cold
- snowman
- ski
- ice skate
- sled
- jacket
- hat
- mittens
- scarf
- boots
- earmuffs

Literature Connection:
It's Winter by Linda Glaser
When Winter Comes by Nancy Van Laan
The Jacket I Wear in the Snow by Shirley Neitzel
Dear Rebecca, Winter Is Here by Jean Craighead George
Winter: Discovering the Season by Louis Sentry

Modeled Writing (sample)
In *winter* it is very cold. Sometimes it *snows*. It is important to wear a *jacket, mittens,* a *hat* and *earmuffs* to keep warm. We can build a *snowman* and go *sledding* in the *snow*.

Teaching Points
- Compound words (snowman, earmuffs)
- *-old* words (cold, hold, fold)
- *-ow* (long o) (snow, low, show)
- Review/highlight sight words

Springboards for Writing
In winter…
I wear…
A snowman is…
Snowflakes are…

Christmas Words

- celebrate
- family
- present
- gift
- tree
- decorate
- ornaments
- sing
- carols
- Santa Claus
- cards
- lights

Literature Connection
Polar Express by Chris van Allsburg
Christmas Around the World by Mary D. Lankford
Children Around the World Celebrate Christmas by Susan T. Osborn
Santa's Short Suit Shrunk and Other Christmas Tongue Twisters by Nola Buck
Max's Christmas by Rosemary Wells

Modeled Writing (sample)
People *celebrate Christmas* in many ways around the world. We *decorate trees* with beautiful *ornaments* and *sing Christmas carols*. I like to exchange *gifts* with my friends and *family*.

Teaching Points
- Clap multi-syllabic words (Christmas, decorate, ornaments)
- *-ee* words (tree, free, see, bee)
- *-ing* words (sing, ring)
- Highlight/review sight words

Springboards for Writing
Christmas is…
Our family celebrates…
I like to decorate…
I am going to give…

Hanukkah Words

- Festival of Lights
- eight days
- Jewish
- family
- menorah
- Shamash
- dreidel
- gelt
- potato latkes
- holiday
- candles
- celebrate
- gifts

Literature Connection
Sammy Spiders' First Hanukkah
  by Sylvia A. Rouss
*Festival of Lights: The Story of
  Hanukkah* by Madia Silverman
The Chanukkah Guest
  by Eric. A. Kimmel
The Trees of the Dancing Goats
  by Patricia Polacco

Modeled Writing (sample)
Hanukkah is the *Jewish* holiday of the *Festival of Lights*. For eight days we light *candles* on the *menorah*. The middle candle is called the *shamash*. We eat *potato latkes* and play the *dreidel* game.

Teaching Points
- Clap multi-syllabic words (festival, menora)
- *-ight* words (light, night)
- Review/highlight sight words

Springboards for Writing
Hanukkah is…
The dreidle game is…
Potato latkes are…
I like…
We light the…

Santa Words

- Santa Claus
- Mrs. Claus
- North Pole
- elves
- presents
- reindeer
- Rudolph
- sleigh
- beard
- Merry Christmas
- chimney
- toys
- workshop

Literature Connection
The Santa Claus Book
  by Alden Perkes
A Letter to Santa
  by Brigitte Weninger
Who'll Pull Santa's Sleigh Tonight
  by Laura Rader
Rudolph Shines Again
  by Robert L. May
When Will Santa Come?
  by Harriet Ziefert
Thank You Santa by Margaret Wila

Modeled Writing (sample)
Santa and *Mrs. Claus* live at the *North Pole*. The *elves* make the *presents* for *Santa* to deliver to the children in his *sleigh*. *Rudolph* and the *reindeer* pull the *sleigh* for *Santa*. *Santa* says, "Ho ho ho, Merry Christmas!"

Teaching Points
- Mrs./Mr./Ms.
- Quotation marks
- Capital letters for names
- Review/highlight sight words

Springboards for Writing
Santa is...
The elves...
Rudolph and the reindeer...
Santa and Mrs. Claus live...
Santa wears...

Toy Words

- puzzle
- doll
- bike
- scooter
- jump rope
- checkers
- trucks
- roller skates
- blocks
- cars
- books
- board game
- play
- friend
- toy box

Literature Connection:
Clown by Quentin Blake
Williams Doll by Charlotte Zolotow
Ira Sleeps Over by Bernard Waber
The Velveteen Rabbit
  by Margery Williams
Grandma's Special Toy Box
  by Rosemary Reuille Irons

Modeled Writing (sample)
Sometimes it's fun to open up my *toy box* and *play* with the first *toy* I pull out. I might *play* with *cars* and *trucks*, a *doll*, or a *puzzle* I got for my birthday. *Toys* are great!

Teaching Points
- Toy rhyming words (boy, joy)
- Initial sounds /t/ and /p/
- Review/highlight sight words
- Highlight word list

Springboards for Writing
My favorite toy is…
My friends like to play…
I sleep with…
For my birthday I got…

Home Words

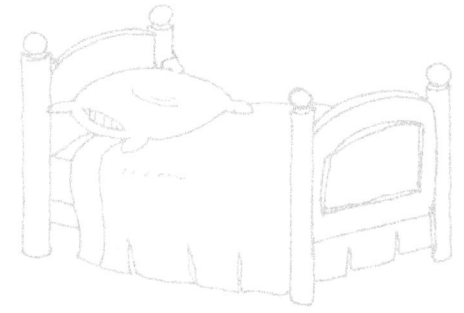

- kitchen
- dining room
- bedroom
- bed
- family room
- television
- bathroom
- den
- couch
- chair
- fireplace
- backyard
- telephone
- computer
- family

Literature Connection
The Little House by Virginia Lee Burton
The House That Jack Built by Jeanette Winter
Little Red Riding Hood by Trina Schart Hyman
Make Way For Ducklings by Robert McCloskey
Goodnight Moon by Margaret Wise Brown

Modeled Writing (sample)
At home my *family* is busy. We take turns cleaning the *kitchen* and *bathroom*s. We make our *bed*s every day. After dinner, we play games in the *family room* until it's time for *bed*.

Teaching Points
- /oo/ sound (room, moon, spoon, zoom)
- -ed words (bed, fed, red)
- Review/highlight sight words
- Highlight list words

Springboards for Writing
My home is…
When I'm at home…
My jobs around the house…
My family likes to…

January Words

- new year
- winter
- hibernate
- sleep
- cold
- snow
- snowman
- celebrate
- resolution
- promise
- Martin Luther King Jr.
- month

Literature Connection
A Busy Year by Leo Lionni
Time to Sleep by Denise Fleming
New Year's Day by Mari C. Schuh
Cold Little Duck, Duck, Duck
  by Lisa Westberg Peters
What Do Animals Do in Winter?
  by Melvin Berger

Modeled Writing (sample)
Happy *New Year*! In *January* we welcome in a *new year*. Many people make a *resolution*, or *promise* to do something better in *January*. What will your *New Year's resolution* be?

Teaching Points
- Capitalize month/holiday
- Question mark usage
- Review/highlight sight words
- Highlight list words

Springboards for Writing
This year I will...
In January I like to ...
My resolution this year is...
My family celebrates the new
   year by...

Snow Words

- cold
- white
- freezing
- powdery
- crunchy
- hills
- mountains
- ski
- snowboard
- sled
- snowflakes
- snowman
- storm
- fall
- snow angels
- snowballs

Literature Connection
Dream Snow by Eric Carle
Snow Ponies by Cynthia Cotton
It's Snowing by Oliver Dunrea
The Mitten by Jan Brett
The First Snowfall
    by Anne F. Rockwell
The Snowy Day by Ezra Jack Keats

Modeled Writing (sample)
Snow is *cold* and *white* and fun to play in! We like to build a *snowman* and make *snow angels* in the snow. Sometimes we go to the mountains to *ski* or *snowboard*. There are so many ways to have fun in the *snow*!

Teaching Points
- Compound words (snowman, snowboard, snow flake)
- *sn* blends (snow, snake, snap)
- Review/highlight sight words
- Highlight list words

Springboards for Writing
Snow is…
When we play in the snow…
My favorite winter sport is…
In the snow I like to …
My snowman has…

Arctic Words

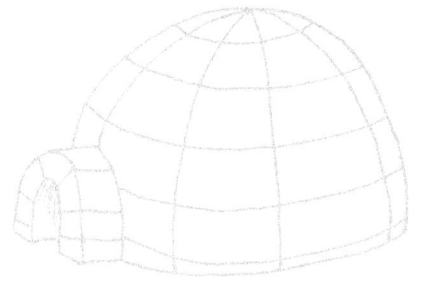

North Pole
polar bear
Eskimo
seal
walrus
ice
South Pole
penguins
fish
snow
cold
frozen
whales
igloo
Antarctic

Literature Connection
Penguins by Gail Gibbons
Arctic Lights, Arctic Nights
  by Debbie S. Miller
Eyewitness: Arctic & Antarctic
  by Barbara Taylor
Little Polar Bear by Hans De Beer
The Polar Bear Son: An Inuit Tale
  by Lydia Dabcovich

Modeled Writing (sample)
Polar bears and *penguins* can never meet! *Polar bears* live in the *Arctic* in the *north* and *penguins* live in the *Antarctic* in the *south*. They both like the *cold frozen* world they live in, but they live at opposite ends of the earth!

Teaching Points
- Initial /p/ sound
- Capitalize places
- /ar/ sound (Arctic, are, art)
- Review/highlight sight words
- Highlight list words

Springboards for Writing
In the Arctic I would see…
If I could have a penguin for a pet…
In the Antarctic I would bring…
Antarctica is so cold…

Whale Words

- ocean
- swim
- mammals
- migrate
- dolphin
- krill
- fish
- orca
- Shamu
- spout
- blowhole
- flippers
- tail
- pod
- toothed
- baleen

Literature Connection
Humphrey the Lost Whale
    by Richard Hall, et al
Baby Beluga (Raffi Songs to Read)
    by Raffi
The Whales' Song by Dyan Sheldon
Baby Whales Drink Milk (Let's-Read-and-Find-Out Science 1)
    by Barbara Juster Esbensen
Is a Blue Whale the Biggest Thing There Is? by Robert E. Wells

Modeled Writing (sample)
Whales are amazing animals! They are *mammals* like you and me, but they live in the *ocean*. They breathe air through a *blowhole* and *swim* with big *flippers* and a *tail*. They *swim* in groups called *pods*. A *pod* is like a whale's family.

Teaching Points
- *wh* digraph
- Ending *th* digraph (breathe, teeth, north)
- Review/highlight sight words
- Highlight list words

Springboards for Writing
Whales are…
A baleen whale…
The blue whale…
My favorite whale is…
Whales live…

Martin Luther King Jr. Words

- Atlanta
- minister
- Corretta Scott King
- Black Americans
- Washington D.C.
- speech
- dream
- freedom
- equality
- rights

Literature Connection
Martin's Big Words: The Life of Dr. Martin Luther King, Jr.
   by Doreen Rappaport
Meet Martin Luther King, Jr.
   by James T. DeKay
I Have a Dream
   by Dr. Martin Luther King Jr.
A Picture Book of Martin Luther King
   by David A. Adler
Martin Luther King Day
   by Linda Lowery

Modeled Writing (sample)
Martin Luther King Jr. fought for *freedom* and *equality* for *Black Americans*. He gave an important speech in *Washington D.C.* The *speech* was called "I Have a Dream."

Teaching Points
- Capitalize names
- *-ee* words (speech, freedom)
- *-ea* words (dream, team, means)
- Review/highlight sight words

Springboards for Writing
Martin Luther King was…
Black Americans…
I have a dream…
Freedom means…
Equality means…

Transportation Words

- travel
- car
- truck
- bus
- taxi
- motorcycle
- trolley
- bike
- bicycle
- airplane
- train
- boat
- ship
- people

Literature Connection
Big Book of Things That Go by Caroline Bingham
Go Dog Go by P.D. Eastman
Machines at Work by Byron Barton
Freight Train by Donald Crews
Wheels on the Bus by Raffi

Modeled Writing (sample)
There are many ways to *travel*. Some people *travel* by *car* and some ride a *motorcycle*. *Airplanes* can take us to faraway places. *Ships* travel across oceans. Have you ever ridden on a *train*?

Teaching Points
- *tr* blend (travel, train, truck)
- Compound words (motorcycle, airplane)
- *-ike* words (bike, hike)
- Review/highlight sight words

Springboards for Writing
My family traveled…
We went on …
I like to ride…
I've never been on a…
The train…

Size Words

- big
- huge
- large
- small
- little
- tiny
- short
- tall
- fat
- skinny
- thin
- average
- heavy
- light

Literature Connection
Big and Little by Steve Jenkins
Is It Larger? Is It Smaller by Tana Hoban
How Big is a Foot? by Rolf Myller
Actual Size by Steve Jenkins
Big Dog...Little Dog: A Bedtime Story by P.D. Eastman

Modeled Writing (sample)
Things come in all *sizes*. A truck is *big*. A building is *huge*. A red ant is *tiny*. Some dogs are *little*. Trees are *tall*. But you are just right!

Teaching Points
- Initial /b/ and /t/ sounds
- Rhyming words with *big* (dig, wig, pig)
- Review/highlight sight words
- Highlight list words

Springboards for Writing
I am as tall as...
A bug is small, but a...
He is bigger than...
Some dinosaurs were...
The little...

February Words

- hearts
- valentine
- love
- friends
- Cupid
- flowers
- hug
- kiss
- candy
- birthday
- Valentine's Day
- George Washington
- Abraham Lincoln
- presidents
- month

Literature Connection
Best Friends for Frances
    by Russell Hoban
My Happy Heart by Melody Carlson
Do You Want to Be My Friend?
    by Eric Carle
Will I Have a Friend?
    by Miriam Cohen
Just Like Abraham Lincoln
    by Bernard Waber

Modeled Writing (sample)
In *February* we think about special people. We honor two American *presidents, Abraham Lincoln* and *George Washington*. This month we also show how much we care by giving *valentines* to our *friends* and family on *Valentine's Day*.

Teaching Points
- Capitalize names/months
- Initial sound /f/
- Review/highlight sight words
- Highlight list words

Springboards for Writing
February is going to be…
Valentine's Day is…
Abraham Lincoln wore…
George Washington taught me…

Valentine's Day Words

love
heart
red
pink
lace
friend
like
hug
kiss
card
envelope
cupid
arrow
kind
nice
poems

Literature Connection
One Zillion Valentines
    by Frank Modell
The Missing Tarts by B.G. Hennessey
Valentine's Day by Miriam Nerlove
The Very Special Valentine
    by Maggie Kneen
The Day It Rained Hearts
    by Felicia Bond

Modeled Writing (sample)
This *Valentine's Day*, I want to make my *valentines*. First, I will need lots of *pink* and *red* paper. Then, I'll decorate them with *lace* and draw pictures of *hearts* and *flowers*. Finally, I will write *kind* words to *friends like* you!

Teaching Points
• Ordering words (first, then, finally)
• Comma usage
• Review/highlight sight words
• Highlight list words
• Meanings of *like*

Springboards for Writing
I want to give valentines to…
On Valentine's Day I will wear…
I like…
Cupid reminds me to…
Love is…

Friend Words

- nice
- like
- play
- best
- help
- fair
- share
- together
- disagree
- argue
- fight
- make-up
- apologize
- smile
- laugh

Literature Connection
Jessica by Kevin Henkes
Odd Velvet by Mary E Whitcomb
Franklin's New Friend
　by Paulette Bourgeois
King of the Playground
　by Phyllis Reynolds Naylor
The Recess Queen by Alexis O'Neill

Modeled Writing (sample)
Friends can make every day great! *Friends share* with each other and have fun while they *laugh* and *play*. Sometimes *friends disagree* and even get into *fights* but they always *make-up* and continue being *friends*.

Teaching Points
- *fr* blend words (friend, freight, frown)
- *sh* digraph words (share, shell, shoe)
- Review/highlight sight words
- Highlight list words

Springboards for Writing
My friend is...
We like to...
Sometimes we play...
Friends can...

Feelings Words

- happy
- glad
- surprised
- sad
- angry
- shy
- mad
- excited
- bored
- proud
- afraid
- silly
- worried
- frustrated
- brave
- courageous

Literature Connection
Lilly's Purple Plastic Purse by Kevin Henkes
100th Day Worries by Margery Cuyler
When Sophie Gets Angry-Really, Really, Angry… by Molly Bang
Today I Feel Silly And Other Moods That Make My Day by Jamie Lee Curtis
My Many Colored Days by Dr. Seuss

Modeled Writing (sample)
Sometimes I *feel happy* and sometimes *sad*. When I try really hard at something and it works, I *feel proud* of what I have done. If something makes me *mad* or *angry*, I count to ten to *feel* better. How do you *feel* today?

Teaching Points
- Question mark usage
- *-ad* words (sad, mad, pad, had)
- Review/highlight sight words
- Highlight list words

Springboards for Writing
I feel happy when…
My sister/brother makes me feel…
I get angry when…
I like to feel…

Post Office Words

- mail
- letter
- mailbox
- mail carrier
- postal worker
- stamps
- envelope
- address
- postcard
- package
- mail
- send
- house
- deliver

Literature Connection
The Jolly Postman by Janet Ahlberg and Allan Ahlberg
A Letter to Amy by Ezra Jack Keats
The Post Office Book by Gail Gibbons
Mail and How It Moves by Gail Gibbons
Good-bye, Curtis by Kevin Henkes

Modeled Writing (sample)
The *post office* is a very busy place. *Postal workers* help people *stamp* and *address envelopes* so they can be sent. *Mail carriers deliver letters* and *packages* to people all over town. I hope I get a special *letter* in my *mailbox* today.

Teaching Points
- Long and short /o/ sound (post, hope, office, box)
- Initial /p/ sound (postal, packages)
- Review/highlight sight words
- Highlight list words

Springboards for Writing
When I get a letter I …
The mail carrier helps…
Sending mail is…
Getting mail is…
I want to write a letter to…

Abraham Lincoln Words

- president
- United States
- slavery
- Civil War
- Illinois
- Kentucky
- Mary Todd Lincoln
- beard
- stove top hat
- log cabin

Literature Connection
A Picture Book of Abraham Lincoln by David A. Adler
Abe Lincoln's Hat by Martha Brenner
Abe Lincoln: The Boy Who Loved Books by Kay Winter
Abraham Lincoln by Ingri D'Aulaire
Abe Lincoln Remembers by Ann Turner

Modeled Writing (sample)
Abraham Lincoln was born in a *log cabin* in *Kentucky*. He loved to read when he was young. He grew up to become *president* of the *United States*. He wore a *stove top hat* and had a *beard*. He signed a law to end *slavery*.

Teaching Points
- Capital letters for names and places
- Clap multi-syllable words (president, Kentucky)
- /o/ words (top, Todd)
- Review/highlight sight words

Springboards for Writing
Abraham Lincoln was…
Abraham Lincoln lived…
He wore…
President Lincoln is known for…

George Washington Words

president
United States
first
country
Martha Washington
Mt. Vernon
general
three-cornered hat
Yankee Doodle
cherry tree
axe
father
lie
wooden teeth

Literature Connection
A Picture Book of George Washington by David Adler
George Washington and the General's Dog by Frank Murphy
George Washington's Breakfast by Jean Fritz
George Washington's Teeth by Deborah Chandra
George Washington: A Picture Book Biography by James Biblin

Modeled Writing (sample)
George Washington was the first *president* of the *United States*. He and his wife, *Martha*, lived in their home called *Mt. Vernon*. There is a story people tell about *George* as a boy. His father asked if he had cut down a *cherry tree* with his *axe*. *George* told his father he did. He would not tell a *lie*.

Teaching Points
- Capitalize names/places
- Abbreviations (Mt., St. Ave.)
- -st endings (first, last, fast)
- Review/highlight sight words

Springboards for Writing
President Washington is remembered for...
If I become president...
The father of our country means...
George Washington was...

March Words

- windy
- sunny
- warm
- spring
- green
- flowers
- growing
- lion
- lamb
- kites
- St. Patrick's Day
- leprechauns
- month

Literature Connection
Turtle Spring by Deborah Turney Zagwyn
My Spring Robin by Anne Rockwell
Countdown to Spring!: An Animal Counting Book by Janet Schulman
O'Sullivan Stew: A Tale Cooked Up in Ireland by Hudson Talbott
One Windy Wednesday by Phyllis Root

Modeled Writing (sample)
When *March* arrives, the weather will *warm* up and things will start to *grow*. This *month* we'll see leaves *growing* back on bare trees. On *windy* days we can fly our *kites*. Best of all, in *March* we always need to watch for a *leprechaun* hiding in the *green* grass!

Teaching Points
- Initial /w/ and /m/ sounds (warm, month)
- /ch/ endings (March, watch, search)
- Review/highlight sight words
- Highlight list words

Springboards for Writing
I like March because…
March is a good month for…
This month I will…
March's weather is …

Spring Words

- warm
- rain
- raindrop
- rainbow
- flowers
- birds
- worm
- babies
- nest
- garden
- planting
- growing
- season

Literature Connection
Spring: An Alphabet Acrostic
   by Steven Schnur
Spring's Sprung by Lynn Plourde
It's Spring by Samantha Berger
Wake Up, It's Spring!
   by Lisa Campbell Ernst
Spring Is Here by Taro Gomi

Modeled Writing (sample)
Spring is here and with it comes *warm* days and new life! This *season* brings *baby birds* hatching in their *nests*. It's also a good time to *plant* seeds in your *garden* and watch them *grow*.

Teaching Points
- Ending /tch/ sound (hatch, watch, itch)
- -ing endings (spring, bring, hatching)
- Exclamation mark usage
- Review/highlight sight words
- Highlight list words

Springboards for Writing
When spring comes…
Spring is a good time to…
In spring, my family…
During spring, birds…
My favorite season is…

Weather Words

- sunny
- cloudy
- rainy
- snow
- windy
- foggy
- cold
- warm
- hot
- breezy
- stormy
- wet
- hail
- thunder
- lightning

Literature Connection
Bringing the Rain to Kapiti Plain by Verna Aardema
The Cloud Book by Tomie dePoala
What Will the Weather Be Like Today? by Paul Rogers
Wild Weather Soup by Caroline Formby
Cloudy With a Chance of Meatballs by Judi Barrett

Modeled Writing (sample)
This week the *weather* has been mostly *sunny*. On *sunny* days, I like to take walks. On *windy* days, it's fun to run and fly my kite. There are fun things to do in every kind of *weather*.

Teaching Points
- Locate short /u/ words
- Locate beginning /w/ sound
- Review/highlight sight words
- Highlight list words

Springboards for Writing
On rainy days I...
My favorite weather is...
When it's too hot/cold, I...
When the rain falls, it sounds...
Sunny/Rainy weather is good for...

Kite Words

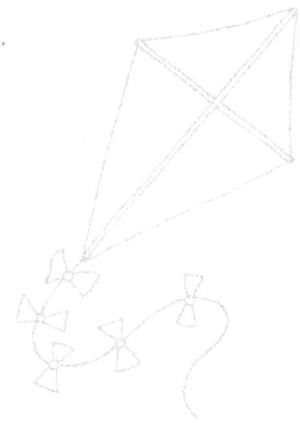

- air
- sky
- fly
- sail
- float
- dance
- run
- string
- tail
- shape
- box
- diamond
- dragon
- fancy

Literature Connection
Kite Flying by Grace Lin
Kites by Hitz Demi
The Emperor and the Kite by Jane Yolen
Curious George Flies a Kite by H.A. Rey
One Monday by Amy Huntington

Modeled Writing (sample)
Kites come in all *shapes* and sizes. The *box kite* has four straight sides. The *dragon kite* has a long *fancy tail*. No matter which kind you like, you'll love seeing your *kite dance* across the *sky* but hold on tight to the *string*!

Teaching Points
- Initial /k/ sound (kite, kind)
- Long /i/ sound (kite, like)
- Review/highlight sight words
- Highlight list words

Springboards for Writing
My kite flies…
Kites are…
Sometimes flying a kite can be…
One time my kite…

St. Patrick's Day Words

Ireland
Irish
leprechaun
green
four-leaf clover
shamrock
Blarney Stone
good luck
rainbow
lucky
pot of gold
trap
catch

Literature Connection
St. Patrick's Day by Gail Gibbons
St. Patrick's Day in the Morning by Eve Bunting
Jack and the Leprechaun by Ivan Robertson
Lucky O'Leprechaun by Jana Dillon
Leprechaun Gold by Teresa Bateman

Modeled Writing (sample)
The *Irish* believe that a *four-leaf clover* brings *good luck*. They say that *leprechauns* have a *pot of gold* at the end of a *rainbow*. They move their *pot of gold* so no one can find it. We can make a *trap* to try to catch a *Leprechaun*.

Teaching Points
- *-uck* words (luck, duck, tuck)
- *-ot* words (pot, hot, dot)
- Review/highlight sight words
- Highlight list words

Springboards for Writing
Leprechauns are…
I am lucky because…
My trap will…
A pot of gold…

Green Words

- color
- grass
- plant
- leaves
- trees
- bamboo
- jungle
- parrots
- bugs
- caterpillar
- grasshoppers
- frogs
- turtles
- alligators
- pickles
- limes

Literature Connection
Verdi by Janell Cannon
Gus and the Green Thing by Janet Reich
Colors by Robert Crowther *Are You a Grasshopper?* by Judy Allen
Five Green and Speckled Frogs by Priscilla Burris
Little Blue and Little Yellow by Leo Lionni

Modeled Writing (sample)
Green is a cool calm *color*. You see it in the big wet *leaves* of the *jungle*. You see *green* on the back of a *turtle's* shell, or when you roll down a *green grassy* hill. Where do you see *green*?

Teaching Points
- Long /e/ sound (green, leaves, see)
- Initial /g/ and /c/ sound
- Review/highlight sight words
- Highlight list words

Springboards for Writing
When I see green, I feel…
My favorite shade of green is…
A yummy green vegetable is…
My favorite color is…

Rainbow Words

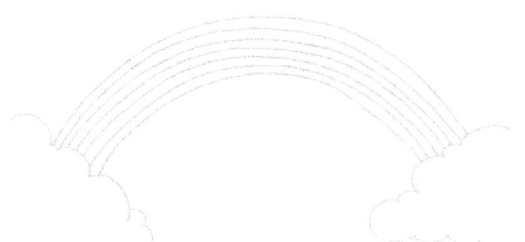

- rain
- sun
- raindrop
- sunlight
- sky
- clouds
- colors
- red
- orange
- yellow
- green
- blue
- indigo
- violet
- beautiful
- colorful
- pot of gold

Literature Connection
All the Colors of the Rainbow
　by Allan Fowler
A Rainbow of my Own
　by Don Freeman
The Rainbow Fish by Marcus Pfister
The Rainbows' Adventure: From
　Raindrops to Rainbows
　by Kimberly Kerr
Moonbear's Skyfire by Frank Asch

Modeled Writing (sample)
You can see a *rainbow* in the *sky* after it *rains*. *Rainbows* are made when *sunlight* passes through *raindrops*. The *colors* of a *rainbow* are *red, orange, yellow, green, blue* and *violet*. *Rainbows* are *beautiful*.

Teaching Points
- Compound words (rainbow, sunlight)
- *-ai* words (rain, train)
- Review/highlight sight words
- Highlight list words

Springboards for Writing
Rainbows are...
I saw a rainbow...
The colors...
My favorite color in the rainbow is...

April Words

spring

warm

sunny

showers

green

flowers

babies

bunny

birds

eggs

nest

growing

Easter

month

Literature Connection
Robins: Songbirds of Spring
　by Mia Posada
Springtime Treasury
　by Sue Barraclough
Fancy That! by Pamela Allen
The Little Rabbit by Judy Dunn
Play With Me by Marie Hall

Modeled Writing (sample)
April is alive with new *growth* everywhere! This *month* we will see new *baby birds* hatching from their *eggs*. The plants will begin to grow new *green* leaves. Maybe the *Easter bunny* will arrive with *eggs* for all!

Teaching Points
- Long /a/ and /e/ sounds (April, baby, maybe, Easter)
- Capitalize months/holidays
- Review/highlight sight words
- Highlight list words

Springboards for Writing
This month I…
In April we celebrate…
One time I saw a nest…
On Easter my family…

Easter Words

- family
- dinner
- eggs
- decorate
- hide
- hunt
- dye
- color
- bunny
- basket
- grass
- chocolate
- parade

Literature Connection
The Easter Bunny that Overslept
  by Pricilla Friedrich
Easter Mice by Bethany Roberts
The Night before Easter
  by Natasha Wing
Owen's Marshmallow Chick
  by Kevin Henkes
Bunny Trouble by Hans Wilhelm

Modeled Writing (sample)
We get ready for Easter by *decorating* eggs. We use crayons to draw pictures on them, like a *bunny* in the *grass*. Then we dip them in bright *dyes* for extra *color*. On Easter day, we *hide* the *eggs* and all the children *hunt* for them. Easter egg hunts are so much fun!

Teaching Points
- Highlight initial sound /d/ and /b/ words
- Short /e/ sound (egg, ready, get)
- Review/highlight sight words
- Highlight list words

Springboards for Writing
Our family…
The Easter Bunny…
On Easter we…
Easter eggs are fun to…

Egg Words

birds
fish
reptiles
hatch
fly
crawl
swim
decorate
lay
deliver
female
mother
nest
shell
round
smooth
bumpy
rough

Literature Connection
An Extraordinary Egg, by Leo Lionni
Green Eggs and Ham by Dr. Seuss
Chickens Aren't the Only Ones
   by Ruth Heller
Seven Eggs by Meredith Hooper
The Most Wonderful Egg in the World!
   by Helme Heine

Modeled Writing (sample)
All kinds of animals *hatch* from eggs. We know *birds* do, but did you know that *reptiles* like snakes and turtles also hatch from eggs? *Fish* even *lay* eggs as well!

Teaching Points
- *-tch* words (hatch, catch, pitch, stitch)
- Locate short /e/ words (eggs, well, reptiles)
- Review/highlight sight words
- Highlight list words

Springboards for Writing
When eggs hatch…
Not all eggs are…
Decorating eggs is…
Once I found a nest…

Bunny Words

- rabbits
- hares
- furry
- soft
- fuzzy
- pink
- hopper
- cotton tail
- legs
- ears
- whiskers
- eyes
- nose
- feet
- carrots
- grass
- burrow
- warren
- babies
- Easter

Literature Connection
The Runaway Bunny
   by Margaret Wise Brown
*The Country Bunny and the Little
   Gold Shoes* by Dubose Heyward
Bunny and Me
   by Adele Aron Greenspun
Home for a Bunny
   by Margaret Wise Brown
Rabbits, Rabbits, and More Rabbits!
   by Gail Gibbons

Modeled Writing (sample)
Bunnies are good *hoppers*. They have long *ears* and *whiskers*, *pink eyes* and a *pink nose*. The best thing about *bunnies* is how *soft* and *furry* they feel! I love *bunnies*!

Teaching Points
- Short /u/ sound
- -*y* ending (bunny, furry, funny)
- Review/highlight sight words
- Highlight list words

Springboards for Writing
Bunnies are...
If I had a pet rabbit...
Bunnies can...
Rabbits live...

Farm Words

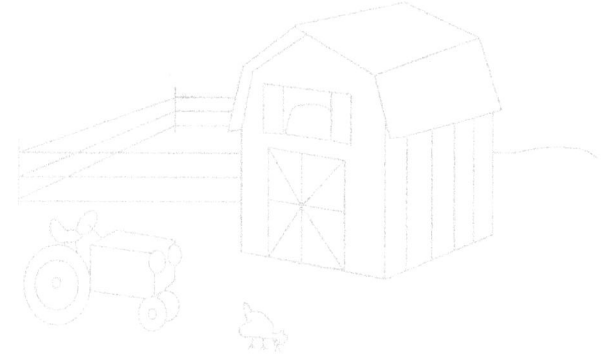

- country
- farmer
- tractor
- plow
- barn
- haystack
- silo
- scarecrow
- field
- crops
- vegetables
- fruit
- wheat
- corn
- garden
- fence
- grow
- planting
- harvest
- pick

Literature Connection
Farming by Gail Gibbons
Rosie's Walk by Pat Hutchins
The Rusty, Trusty Tractor
  by Joy Cowley
Farmer Duck by Matrin Waddell
Dora's Eggs by Julie Sykes

Modeled Writing (sample)
Most *farms* are in the *country*. *Farmers* use a *tractor* to *plow* the *fields* before they plant their *crops* and *gardens*. *Farmers* grow *crops* such as *corn* and *wheat*. The farmer's *tractor* and *tools* are kept in the *barn*.

Teaching Points
- *-ar* words (farm, farmer, barn, garden)
- *pl* blend (plant, plow)
- Review/highlight sight words
- Highlight list words

Springboards for Writing
Farmers grow…
In the barn there are…
Tractors help…
A farm is…

Farm Animals Words

- cow
- horse
- pig
- sheep
- chicken
- rooster
- hen
- barnyard
- coop
- pen
- cock-a doodle doo
- moo
- oink

Literature Connection
Old MacDonald Had a Farm by Glen Rounds
Baby Farm Animals by Garth Williams
The Noisy Farm – Lots of Animal Noises to Enjoy by Marni McGee
Click, Clack, Moo: Cows That Type by Doreen Cronin
Cock-A-Doodle-Doo! Barnyard Hullabaloo by Giles Andreae

Modeled Writing (sample)
"Cock-a-doodle-doo," says the *rooster* as he wakes up the *animals* in the *barnyard*. The *pigs* in the pen say "*oink*" and the *cows* answer with a loud "*moo.*" The *chickens* and *hens* in the *coop* are waiting to be fed. *Farm animals* can be very noisy!

Teaching Points
- Highlight quotation marks for dialogue
- /oo/ sound (rooster, doodle-doo, moo, coop)
- -en words (pen, hen)
- Highlight/review sight words

Springboards for Writing
A rooster says…
The pigs…
Cows…
My favorite farm animal is…

Pet Words

dog
puppy
cat
kitten
rabbit
bunny
bird
parrot
fish
guinea pig
hamster
snake
turtle
food
dish
bowl
cage
kennel
doghouse
vet
play

Literature Connection
The Best Pet of All by David LaRochell
Emma's Pet by David M. McPhail
Clifford the Big Red Dog
　by Norman Bridwell
I Will Always Love You
　by Hans Wilhelm
The Perfect Pet by Margie Palatini
What about my Goldfish?
　by Lillian Hoban

Modeled Writing (sample)
We have lots of *pets*. My sister has a *cat* and two *fish*. I have a *turtle* and a *guinea pig*. Our family has a *dog* named Buddy. We take good care of our *pets*.

Teaching Points
- *-et* words (pet, set, met)
- *-og* words (dog, hog, log)
- *-ish* words (fish, dish, wish)
- Review/highlight sight words

Springboards for Writing
My dog likes to...
One time my cat...
My pet's name is...
I like to play with my...

May Words

- month
- spring
- warm
- sunny
- flowers
- insects
- bloom
- growing
- blossom
- green
- mother
- special
- mom

Literature Connection
A Day with May by Nat Gabriel
Will You Be My Friend? A Bunny and Bird Story by Nancy Tafuri
A Mother for Choco by Keiko Kasza
The Reason for a Flower by Ruth Heller
Flower Garden by Eve Bunting

Modeled Writing (sample)
May is here! All of May's *flowers* are in full *bloom*. The *warm spring* days bring out the *blossoms* on every plant. This *month*, I think I'll give some *flowers* to my *mom*.

Teaching Points
- *-ing* words (spring, bring)
- Long /a/ sound (May, days)
- Rhyming words for May (say, play, day)
- Highlight list words

Springboards for Writing
This month is good for…
In May, I go to…
My mom loves May because…
Flowers are …

Mother's Day Words

- mom
- love
- special
- flowers
- hugs
- kisses
- share
- family
- present
- gift
- card
- breakfast
- lunch
- dinner

Literature Connection
Mother's Day Mice by Eve Bunting
A Chair for My Mother
   by Vera B. Williams
Are You My Mother?
   by Philip D. Eastman
Mother's Day by Anne Rockwell
Mama, Do You Love Me?
   by Barbara M. Joosse

Modeled Writing (sample)
I *love* my *mom*. On her *special* day, I will bring her *breakfast* in bed. I won't forget to tell her how much I *love* her and give her a big *kiss* and *hug*! She is the best!

Teaching Points
- Short /e/ words (special, bed, tell)
- Initial /b/ sounds (best, bed, bring)
- Highlight/review sight words
- Highlight list words

Springboards for Writing
My mom likes to…
This Mother's Day, I will…
One time my mom…
I love my mom because…

Job Words

- teacher
- doctor
- musician
- dentist
- cashier
- mechanic
- nurse
- scientist
- pilot
- builder
- firefighter
- mail carrier
- lawyer
- veterinarian
- police officer

Literature Connection
Jobs People Do
    by Christopher Maynard
My Dad's Job by Peter Glassman
Career Day by Anne Rockwell
I Want to be a Vet
    by Daniel Liebman
Busy, Busy Town by Richard Scarry

Modeled Writing (sample)
Both my mom and dad have a *job*. My dad is a *mechanic*. He fixes cars and trucks. My mom is a *nurse* and works in a hospital. She wears a uniform and helps people who are sick. What *job* do you want when you grow up?

Teaching Points
- /o/ words (job, dog, top, doctor)
- Compound words (firefighter, mail carrier)
- Review/highlight sight words
- Highlight list words

Springboards for Writing
My mom…
My dad…
When I grow up, I want to be…
Jobs are…

Plant Words

water
soil
sunlight
nutrients
grow
sow
garden
seed
root
leaf
leaves
stem
flower
petal

Literature Connection
How a Seed Grows
    by Helene J. Jordan
The Tiny Seed by Eric Carle
From Seed to Plant by Gail Gibbons
Fruit is a Suitcase for Seeds
    by Jean Richards
The Reason for a Flower
    by Ruth Heller

Modeled Writing (sample)
Plants have many parts. The *roots* carry *nutrients* through the *stem* to the *leaves* and *flower*. *Plants* need *water* and *sunlight* to grow. We are going to grow a *plant* from a *seed* in our *garden*.

Teaching Points
- *pl-* words (plant, play, please)
- *-ee* words (seed, feed)
- *-ow* words (grow, sow, flow)
- Review/highlight sight words

Springboards for Writing
A flower is…
Seeds grow…
Plants need…
My garden is…
We grew…

Vegetable Words

- carrots
- peas
- tomatoes
- broccoli
- celery
- beans
- lettuce
- cauliflower
- brussel sprouts
- asparagus
- potatoes
- avocado
- corn
- grow
- salad

Literature Connection
Growing Vegetable Soup by Lois Elhert
Eating the Alphabet: Fruits and Vegetables from A to Z by Lois Elhert
The Edible Pyramid: Good Eating Every Day by Loreen Leedy
The Great Big Enormous Turnip/The Magic Porridge Pot by Elizabeth Laird
Stone Soup by Ann McGovern

Modeled Writing (sample)
We are going to make *vegetable* soup. We will put *carrots, squash, celery, peas, cauliflower* and *potatoes* in the cooking pot. It will be delicious.

Teaching Points
- Clap multi-syllable words (vegetable, tomatoes, broccoli)
- *-ea* words (peas, beans)
- Review/highlight sight words
- Highlight list words

Springboards for Writing
My favorite vegetable is…
For lunch I like to eat…
Carrots are…
I don't like…
Vegetable soup is…

Zoo Words

zookeeper

trainer

cage

pool

train

entrance

tram

exhibit

tricks

tank

cave

animals

veterinarian

Literature Connection
Zoo by Gail Gibbins
My Visit to the Zoo by Aliki
If I ran the Zoo by Dr. Seuss
If Anything Ever Goes Wrong at the Zoo by Mary Jean Hendrick
Our Class Trip to the Zoo by Shirley Neitzel

Modeled Writing (sample)
The *zookeeper* takes care of all the *animals* in the *zoo*. It is fun to ride the *tram* and see the animals in their homes. I like to watch the polar bears in the *pool* and the monkeys in their *cages*. There are many animal *exhibits* at the zoo. Sometimes you can watch the *trainers* work with the elephants too.

Teaching Points
- *-er* endings (zookeeper, trainer)
- long /a/ sound (cave, cage)
- *-oo* words (zoo, too)
- Highlight/review sight words
- Highlight list words

Springboards for Writing
The zoo is…
My favorite zoo exhibit is…
I like to watch the…
Trainers help…

Zoo Animal Words

giraffe

zebra

monkey

gorilla

snake

bear

alligator

elephant

lion

tiger

bird

kangaroo

rhinoceros

hippo

Literature Connection
Scholastic Encyclopedia of Animals
    by Laurence P. Pringle
Snappy Little Zoo by Derek Matthews
1,2,3, To The Zoo: A Counting Book
    by Eric Carle
Last Night at the Zoo
    by Michael Garland
Going to the Zoo by Tom Paxton

Modeled Writing (sample)
At the *zoo* you can see all kinds of *animals*. I love to watch the *kangaroos* hop. *Giraffes* have very long necks. *Zebras* have black and white stripes and some *snakes* do too. I like to hear the *lions* roar. What is your favorite *zoo animal*?

Teaching Points
- Clap multi-syllable words (animal, elephant, kangaroo)
- *-ake* word families (snake)
- Highlight/review sight words

Springboards for Writing
Monkeys swing...
An elephant is...
Tigers can...
My favorite zoo animal is...

June Words

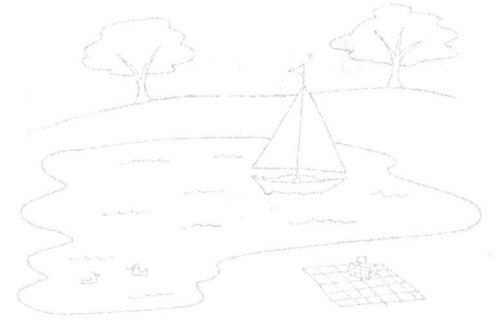

- summer
- sunny
- warm
- beach
- picnic
- holiday
- Father's Day
- month
- celebrate
- play
- special
- pool
- swimming

Literature Connection
How I Spent My Summer Vacation
  by Mark Teague
Mouse's First Summer
  by Lauren Thompson
F is for Flag
  by Wendy Cheyette Lewison
My Dad is Awesome
  by Nick Butterworth
A Perfect Father's Day by Eve Bunting

Modeled Writing (sample)
In the *month* of *June*, we plan lots of *outdoor* things. We like to go to the *beach* when the weather is *warm* and *sunny*. We also celebrate *Father's Day* by having a *picnic* at the *park*. Dad is the *special* person of the day!

Teaching Points
- Locate /p/ and /w/ sounds
- Capitalize months/holidays
- Review/highlight sight words
- Highlight list words

Springboards for Writing
This month my family...
In June I like to ...
My dad is...
For Father's Day we...

Summer Words

sunny
warm
swim
pool
beach
barbeque
yard
sports
friends
read
sprinkler
insects
fan

Literature Connection
Summer by Alice Low
Summer Party by Cynthia Rylant
Come On, Rain by Karen Hesse
Fireflies by Julie Brinckloe
It's Summer by Jimmy Pickering

Modeled Writing (sample)
Summer is finally here! It is time to put on swimsuits and go. Let's go to the park or the pool. Swimming is a fun way to cool down. We can also run through the sprinklers and get wet!

Teaching Points
• Rhyming words (cool, pool, school)
• Locate /s/ and /p/ sounds
• Review/highlight sight words
• Highlight list words

Springboards for Writing
The best thing about summer is…
In summer, we go …
This summer I want to …
My favorite season is…

Beach Words

- ocean
- water
- sand
- waves
- fish
- shells
- seaweed
- sea gull
- sandcastle
- bucket
- shovel
- umbrella
- swimsuit
- sunscreen
- towel
- sailboat

Literature Connection
What Lives in a Shell
   by Kathleen Weidner
Grandma Summer by Harley Jessup
Sea, Sand, Me! by Patricia Hubbell
*A Day at the Beach: A Seaside
   Counting Book from One to Ten*
   by Sandy Seeley Walling
Beach Day by Karen Roosa

Modeled Writing (sample)
Going to the *beach* is always an adventure. We bring an *umbrella* and lots of *sunscreen*. It's fun to make a *sandcastle* and decorate it with *shells* and *seaweed*. We can play and *swim* in the *ocean* and ride the *waves*.

Teaching Points
- Clap multi-syllable words (umbrel-la, sandcastle, adventure)
- Locate /s/ and /sh/ sounds
- Review/highlight sight words
- Highlight list words

Springboards for Writing
At the beach I...
I love the beach because...
One time at the beach I saw a...
I collect...

Sea Life Words

fish
whales
seaweed
octopus
coral
shells
sand
ocean
sharks
clams
crabs
lobster
shore
water
tide pools
sea turtle

Literature Connection
Into the Sea by Brenda Z. Guiberson
A Swim through the Sea
    by Kristin Joy Pratt
A House for Hermit Crab by Eric Carle
Swimmy by Leo Lionni
One Lonely Sea Horse
    by Saxton Freymann

Modeled Writing (sample)
The *ocean* is full of sea life. In the *water*, there are schools of *fish*. Near the *shore*, there are *crabs* and *lobster*. If I dig in the wet *sand*, I can find *clams* too. The *sea* is home to many animals.

Teaching Points
- Long /o/ sound words (ocean, open, only)
- Highlight *cr* blend (crab, crust, cricket, etc.)
- Review/highlight sight words
- Highlight list words

Springboards for Writing
The ocean is full of…
Besides fish, the sea has…
If I had a boat…
Ocean animals are…

Insect Words

- bug
- beetle
- butterfly
- grasshopper
- caterpillar
- bee
- moth
- fly
- worm
- head
- thorax
- abdomen
- wings
- legs
- antenna
- feelers
- fly
- crawl
- wiggle
- metamorphosis
- change
- flower

Literature Connection
Bugs! Bugs! Bugs! by Bob Barner
Bugs are Insects by Anne Rockwell
Caterpillars, Bugs and Butterflies by Mel Boring
Waiting for Wings by Lois Ehlert
The Very Quiet Cricket by Eric Carle

Modeled Writing (sample)
You can find *insects* all around the garden. A *worm* wiggles on the ground and a *bee* buzzes around the plants. I see a *butterfly* rest on the petal of a flower. I like to chase after *grasshoppers*. *Bugs* are fun to watch!

Teaching Points
- Words that rhyme with bug
- Compound words (grasshopper, butterfly)
- Highlight/review sight words
- Highlight list words

Springboards for Writing
I like to catch…
A beetle looks like…
Butterflies are…
Bugs are…

Father's Day Words

dad

daddy

grandfather

papa

love

gift

hug

card

special

celebrate

picnic

barbeque

Literature Connection
I Love My Daddy by Sebastin Braun
A Perfect Father's Day by Eve Bunting
My Dad Is Awesome
  by Nick Butterworth
What Daddies Do Best
  by Laura Numeroff
What Daddy Loves by Sue Kassirer

Modeled Writing (sample)
I *love* my dad. He makes me laugh and gives me *hugs*. He reads to me each night before I go to sleep. For Father's Day, I am going to make him a *card* and buy him a *special gift*.

Teaching Points
- Words that rhyme with dad
- Words that rhyme with hug
- Highlight/review sight words
- Highlight list words

Springboards for Writing
One time my dad…
My daddy is…
Grandfathers…
Fathers are special because…

July Words

- summer
- hot
- sunny
- vacation
- Independence Day
- celebrate
- swim
- picnic
- beach
- camping
- pool
- family
- park
- barbeque
- backyard
- month

Literature Connection
Fourth of July Mice by Bethany Roberts
Mister Seahorse by Eric Carle
Summer Fun by Larry Dane Brimmer
The Great White Man-Eating Shark: A Cautionary Tale by Margaret Mahy
The Cat's Vacation by Irene Schoch

Modeled Writing (sample)
July is a good *month* to play outside and enjoy the *sunny* weather. *Picnics* and *barbeques* are always fun this *month*. We will see a *firework's* show on the fourth to celebrate America's birthday! *July* is great!

Teaching Points
- Ending /th/ digraph (month, fourth)
- Initial /f/ sound (fun, fireworks, fourth)
- Review/highlight sight words
- Highlight list words

Springboards for Writing
In July my family…
July is a good month to…
This month I will…
In the summer…

Fourth of July Words

independence
America
fireworks
red
white
blue
picnic
sparklers
flag
barbeque
parade
celebrate
hamburgers
hotdogs

Literature Connection
Hats Off for the Fourth of July
  by Harriet Ziefert
Fourth of July Mice!
  by Bethany Roberts
Hooray for the Fourth of July
  by Wendy Watson
Apple Pie Fourth of July
  by Janet S. Wong
The Story of America's Birthday
  by Patricia A Pingry

Modeled Writing (sample)
On the *Fourth of July*, we *celebrate America's* day of *Independence*. Our town has a *parade* and everyone dresses in *red, white* and *blue*. We have a *picnic* and dad *barbeques hamburgers* and *hot dogs*. We have *apple pie* for dessert. At night, we watch the *fireworks*.

Teaching Points
- Clap multi-syllabic words (independence, America, barbeque)
- Highlight/review sight words
- Highlight list words

Springboards for Writing
On the Fourth of July we will...
Fireworks are...
We will eat...
The parade will...

Fruit Words

- apple
- orange
- grapefruit
- peach
- banana
- pear
- strawberry
- plum
- pineapple
- lemon
- cherry
- lime
- grape

Literature Connection
Eating the Alphabet: Fruits and Vegetables from A-Z
    by Lous Elhert
Fruit (First Discovery Book)
    by Pascale De Bourgoing
An Alphabet Salad: Fruits and Vegetables from A to Z
    by Sarah L. Schuette
The Bowl of Fruit by Joyce Dunbar
The Little Mouse, the Red Ripe Strawberry, and the Big Hungry Bear by Audrey Wood

Modeled Writing (sample)
Fruit salad is delicious. I like slices of *apples, oranges, bananas, peaches* and *strawberries* in my *fruit salad*. Fresh *fruit* tastes yummy on a hot summer day and it's good for me too!

Teaching Points
- *fr* blend words (fruit, fresh)
- Compound words (strawberry, grapefruit)
- Highlight/review sight words
- Highlight list words

Springboards for Writing
Bananas are fun to eat...
My favorite fruit is...
Grapes grow...
I eat apples with...

Bear Words

- teddy
- stuffed
- cuddly
- soft
- furry
- button eyes
- nose
- paws
- fuzzy
- sleep
- bed

Literature Connection
Ira Sleeps Over by Bernard Waber
The Legend of the Teddy Bear
   by Frank Murphy
Goldilocks and the Three Bears
   by Jan Brett
Corduroy by Don Freeman
Teddy Bears Picnic
   by Jimmy Kennedy

Modeled Writing (sample)
I have a special *teddy* bear that I sleep with every night. His name is Buddy and he is *soft* and *cuddly*. He is a brown bear. He has two *button eyes* and a *nose*. He hugs me with his *paws* and I hug him back!

Teaching Points
- Short /u/ words (hug, cuddly, button, Buddy)
- Capitalize proper names
- Highlight/review sight words
- Highlight list words

Springboards for Writing
My teddy bear is...
Bears are...
I take my teddy bear...
My teddy bear's name is...

Camping Words

- tent
- sleeping bag
- flashlight
- stove
- campfire
- cook out
- marshmallows
- lantern
- mosquitoes
- canoe
- hike
- campout

Literature Connection
Quiet Night by Marilyn Singer
When We Go Camping
 by Margriet Ruurs
Bailey Goes Camping
 by Kevin Henkes
Toasting Marshmallow:
 Camping Poems
 by Kristine O'Connell George *Just Camping Out* by Mercer Mayer

Modeled Writing (sample)
When we *camp*, we sleep in a big *tent*. The last time we went *camping*, we went for a *canoe* ride and we *fished* everyday. At night, we sat around the *campfire* telling stories and roasting *marshmallows*. I can't wait till the next *campout*!

Teaching Points
- *-ing* endings (telling, camping, roasting)
- *–amp* words (camp, lamp, stamp)
- Highlight/review sight words
- Highlight list words

Springboards for Writing
Camping is…
The best part about camping is…
My family camps…
When we camp, I can…

August Words

- summer
- hot
- sunny
- camp
- swim
- play
- picnic
- pool
- friends
- fun
- mosquitoes
- family
- barbeque
- month

Literature Connection
One Hot Summer Day by Nina Crews
Clifford Keeps Cool by Norman Bridwell
Summer Story by Jill Barklem
Hot City by Barbara Joosse
Sun Dance, Water Dance by Jonathan London

Modeled Writing (sample)
August is filled with *hot, sunny* days. It's a good month to spend time visiting *family* and *friends*. We like to *swim* in the *pool* and have a *barbeque* for dinner. In August, we try to stay cool and keep away from the mosquitoes!

Teaching Points
- Capitalize month names
- *-ool* rhyming words (pool, cool, school, tool)
- Review/highlight sight words
- Highlight list words

Springboards for Writing
When it's hot, I…
In August we…
This month my family…
For vacation…

Vacation Words

- summer
- travel
- visit
- camp
- beach
- trip
- mountains
- lake
- desert
- tent
- hotel
- motor home
- airplane

Literature Connection
Summer's Vacation by Lynn Plourde
The Berenstein Bears and Too Much Vacation by Stan and Jan Berenstein
The Best Vacation Ever by Stuart J. Murphy
How I spent My Summer Vacation by Mark Teague
When the Fireflies Come by Jonathan London

Modeled Writing (sample)
This *summer* our family will take a *trip* to the *mountains*. We will *travel* by car. We are going to *camp* and sleep in a *tent*. We will have fun swimming in the *lake*. I can't wait for our *vacation*.

Teaching Points
- *tr* blends (travel, trip)
- Long /a/ words (take, lake)
- Highlight and review sight words
- Highlight list words

Springboards for Writing
This summer…
I am going to visit…
We will travel by…
Our trip to…

Dinosaur Words

- T-Rex
- Brachiosaurus
- Triceratops
- Allosaurus
- Stegosaurus
- Pteranodon
- armor
- claws
- horns
- reptile
- lizard
- meat-eaters
- plant-eaters

Literature Connection
*The Big Book of Dinosaurs:
    A First Book for Young Children*
    by Angela Wilkes
Patrick's Dinosaurs by Carol Carrick
How Do Dinosaurs Say Goodnight?
    by Jane Yolan
Dinosaur Roar! by Paul Strickland
Danny and the Dinosaur by Syd Hoff

Modeled Writing (sample)
Dinosaurs lived a long time ago. *T-Rex* and *Brontosaurus* were two of the biggest *dinosaurs* with strong *claws*. *Triceratops* had three horns on the top of its head. *Stegosaurus* had bony plates down its back. *Pteranodon* was a flying reptile.

Teaching Points
- Listen for the –*saurus* in the names of the dinosaurs
- Capitalize names
- Review/highlight sight words
- Highlight list words

Springboards for Writing
T-Rex is…
Triceratops has…
The strongest dinosaur is…
My favorite dinosaur is…

Five Senses Words

see
hear
taste
smell
touch
sight
eyes
colors
ears
sounds
tongue
flavor
sweet
sour
nose
perfume
stinky
hands
skin
hot
cold
smooth

Literature Connection
Is It Rough? Is It Smooth? Is It Shiny? by Tana Hoban
My Five Senses by Aliki
The Listening Walk by Paul Showers
The Five Senses by Keith Faulkner
Me and My Senses by Joan Sweeney

Modeled Writing (sample)
Our *five senses* help us understand our world. With the *sound* of the doorbell, our *ears* are at work. When we *see* the light turn green, our *sense* of *sight* tells us. When we take a bite of a yummy cookie, our *sense* of *taste* is so happy!

Teaching Points
- List /ou/ words (sound, our, house)
- Highlight initial /s/ and /t/ words (sound, sight, sense, tells, take, taste)
- Review/highlight sight words
- Highlight list words

Springboards for Writing
My five senses help me…
I like to listen to…
At the beach I see…I hear…
I wish everything tasted like…

My Body Words

face
head
neck
shoulders
chest
belly
waist
hips
back
arms
hands
fingers
thumbs
legs
knees
ankle
feet
toes

Literature Connection
Hidden World: Human Body
 by Claude Delafosse
My First Body Book
 by Christopher Rice
Me and My Amazing Body
 by Joan Sweeney
My Body by Lisa Bullard
Parts by Tedd Arnold

Modeled Writing (sample)
Exercise helps my body stay in shape. It makes my *arms* and *legs* strong. It helps me hold my *head* up and keep my *back* straight. Exercise makes me feel good all over.

Teaching Points
- Locate short /e/ words (exercise, helps, legs, head)
- Locate long /a/ words (stay, shape, makes, straight)
- Review/highlight sight words
- Highlight list words

Springboards for Writing
My body lets me...
I am so strong, I can...
I take care of my body by...
When I am bigger...

www.ingramcontent.com/pod-product-compliance
Lightning Source LLC
Chambersburg PA
CBHW081842170426
43199CB00017B/2814